BETWEEN THE LINES

Naho Owada

Author: Naho Owada
Editor and Composition: Julie Rumbarger
Website and Forward by Cyril Colnel

September, 2018.

For information or to book a one on one session with Naho, please see website @ nahoowada.com
ISBN

This book is about nonduality and the falling away of the illusory sense of self (me), also known as enlightenment.

Naho's native language is Japanese, with French and English being something more recently acquired.

Born in Japan, Naho currently lives in Paris and speaks on the subject of nonduality worldwide, as well as giving private sessions online. If you would like to attend a meeting or schedule a session with Naho, visit www.nahoowada.com

Forward

My first knowledge of nonduality came upon meeting Naho. The interest that I had was with her and I felt that if I wanted to show my interest in Naho, I may first try to understand nonduality. I looked on the web and in videos and my first impression was that it was full of words and more words, going round and round in complexities about what I thought was a philosophy; I was bored.

Somehow though, I understood it when Naho spoke. I felt energetically that she was speaking my language. I could not understand why most nonduality speakers used so many words to describe the simplicity of nothing that is even speakable.

I see so often, the same seekers at the same meetings that participate in nonduality and try so hard to find answers but consequently stay blocked at the same level.

I understand that the nonduality message can be powerful but I would say that it is only powerful when the speaker themselves speaks from the place of amazing energy, an energy that Naho expresses every single day.

Naho lives nonduality and it is for me the only way to understand this message.

I respect very much that Naho does not stop answering people during her talks when participants seem to be blocked about some problem. Naho keeps on answering to give them the possibility to change their life and live, as I like to say, in a perfect freedom.

Naho loves life, and her ability to make disappear all the bad things and share her energy with everybody makes me so proud of her.

It is my impression that Naho knows she saves lives and it is her passion.

I saw Naho and Julie write this book every night with so much love. It shows that her passion is in this book and I enjoyed reading it because I felt the same Naho energy in the words.

Cyril
Paris, France

What you are looking for is not knowing. This is not about being awareness, or watching awareness, or consciousness. This is the end of the one who cares about all of that. What this is, is beyond anything you could ever imagine.

When I say that 'you don't exist,' it comes from unconditional love; it is the end of separation.

- Naho -

Meeting Love

People love this message because they touch the purity. All things melt into everything when you meet love. Nothing can compare to this.

This is the calling to what you already know. When you touch this indescribable message, you can't stop; you may turn from it for a moment, but inevitably you return and that is because something knows this. There is a resonating. You find out there is no separation *through* the resonating.

When life is as it is, there is total freedom, total relaxation.

Apparently

It was before the age of one when Naho sensed that humanity, this world, was not a comfortable place. Her mother told her that she first noticed Naho's experience of the world while she was in her baby seat. Naho appeared to be in shock. She said that often her eyes would be wide and moving from left to right, as if she were seeing evil or in terror. Naho was very tense.

Somewhere around the age of three, there was a natural sense that saw clearly the loneliness or suffering underneath people in general. Naho could see in the faces that there was something hiding, an unease underneath the smile. Naho was always feeling uncomfortable.

By the time Naho turned five, she asked her mother why she had to continue to live.

It was in her teen years that she began her deep search in finding the cause of the uncomfortableness, of which she never found.

Around the age of 20, she realized she would not find the answer where she was looking. Naho didn't experience any tragedies in her life and therefore knew that it was not the story of the life that was causing the suffering.

At the age of 25, Naho met a man who had a profound experience of oneness. He told her that the cause of suffering was the phantom self. She began to see that wherever she went, 'there' she would be. It seemed to be following her; this 'I'. She couldn't escape the self that seemed to be having such uncomfortableness. It was from there that she knew she found the answer she was searching for.

It became evident that everyone is born with a sense of lack that comes from an apparent separation--but this has nothing to do with the story of the apparent life. People try to find the answer in their storyline and that is because they think if they change the story, it will bring them happiness. It became very clear to Naho that that is just not true; that it will only bring relief for a short period of time. It began to be obvious that the person we believe our 'self' to be, is a complete illusion. Soon thereafter, there came an apparent moment (while on her way to the organic supermarket) that the illusion completely vanished. What was left is everything, without a center.

Everything naturally already is; the effort of getting there is the dilemma. That energy of effort creates the veil and the hiding of home.

- Naho -

Sense of Lack

The uncomfortableness from the sense of separation comes from the sense of lack. It is the sense of lack that says, "I should be better," "I need to get more information," "I have to figure things out to protect myself." All of this information is telling you, right now, that you are not enough.

When there's a distance between what you think is happening and who you think you are, it creates a sense of lack, because the sense of 'me' feels that what is happening is happening to 'me'.

What you are actually looking for is not getting something in order to cover up the sense of lack but the end of the the separation which is illusory.

There is no distance anywhere; everything is indivisible and the same.

Control Dream

When you go to bed and you dream something, it feels real doesn't it? But it's not actually happening. It is the same thing happening here. What is actually happening, is a dream, an illusion. This dream is an apparent reality for the human.

It is the apparent person who believes that they are in control--that is the dream; the illusion. There is nobody controlling and nobody being controlled. There is no person inside of a body; that's all identification as a body.

This dreamlike reality, this sense of having control becomes real, and more and more, life is serious. I often hear people say that they are disappointed or don't know what to do after hearing the individual has no control. But this message is not saying the individual has no control, this message is saying there is no controller. Everything is happening without the illusory individual.

There is a reality which has no individual doing independently.

It can be shocking to hear that the apparent personal life that you seem to live is a dream for the first time, but when it is seen, it is simple and obvious.

It is possible that this can be revealed.

The only thing you want is the end of separation, the end of the dream.

What is happening is beyond words.

Seriousness

In the natural reality there is no seriousness. It is all appearing and perfectly complete in every way.

From the human view it may appear imperfect, but it's always perfect as it is.

As soon as 'me' feels, "I exist," it becomes the center of the world and the world outside becomes real too. Since everything seems real, then the negative scenes of people dying or tragedies in life or nature become shocking and serious. The life story then becomes more serious in time and 'me' feels it is all happening to 'me'. 'Me' takes it all personally.

This message is pointing to another possibility altogether, where 'me' is illusory.

When me goes, that seriousness collapses.

Me Tendency

Some apparent people identify with a past shock or traumatic experience and that suffering becomes who they are.

They think they are suffering because of a situation or because of something that is happening but that identification is already attached. Suffering is them. "I am a sufferer."

'Me's tendency is to hang on or identify with something.

Apparent Change

When the message begins to be heard, the apparent dissolving-deconstruction happens to an apparent 'me', effortlessly.

Change, when it seemingly happens, happens naturally without anybody's effort. It is an energetic happening, apparently on its own.

Seeking is the 'me' dynamic and it happens naturally. If you try to stop it, that is another form of seeking.

- Naho -

Seeking Fulfillment

The individual, as an apparent separate energy, is trying to find something for 'me', something special that will make 'me' feel fulfilled.

Things like therapy, meditation, and practices, can bring about a relaxation in the next apparent moment but it is not leading anywhere, there is no arrival.

It is the apparent separation that makes it feel as though something is missing. The sense of separation is always on the move, that is the 'me' dynamic. This 'me' dynamic hides what is already here which is everything that was ever longed for. This can be a horrible message for 'me', but it's actually all love.

Teaching

A lot of people who come to my talks that have been seeking for years, often come to me expecting a teaching, giving them something to do. They think that they have to change in order to become good enough to become 'enlightened'.

In teachings, change can apparently happen, but this gives the impression of getting somewhere which is the dream.

'You' are attracted to this message because the dualistic life is not satisfying. It comes from the sense of not being good enough, and leaves an impression that you have to change yourself. That is the suffering.

All dream teachings are dualistic.

True change happens naturally when this message is deeply touched. What you are looking for is beyond that as well because that is still the dream.

Spirituality

This message is not about spiritually or a personal enlightenment story, it is a revealing of the unnatural story of the human.

Often, the foundation of spiritual teachings tell us that if we do this or that, or if we are good etc., we will then be protected. What they are actually doing is covering up the fear (sense of lack) that is already there.

The fear doesn't go away by covering it up with spiritual practices. The uncomfortableness doesn't come from the story of one's life, the uncomfortableness is already there, underneath.

What you are looking for has nothing to do with changing your apparent story. It needs no commitment or effort in trying to be better.

What is actually happening by hearing this message is a natural falling away of the apparent separate energy that wants to be better.

What is left is perfection in any way that it appears. People have so many ideas about perfection when imperfection is of course already perfect.

Intellectual

Understanding

As long as there is a linear teaching of liberation, it is seemingly going in the opposite direction energetically from what already is.

Insights, experiences, and deconstruction is seemingly happening, but the only importance in them is in an awakening story.

What you are truly looking for has nothing to do with a better teaching or getting more knowledge.

You seek to improve your knowledge by moving from teaching to teaching when what I am talking about is the end of needing to know more.

Seeking is the 'me dynamic and it happens naturally. If you try to stop it, that is another form of seeking.

This, is beyond all that you apparently know.

Hope

In the dreamlike reality, hope means that the dream continues.

The apparent person moves by means of hope. Without hope, the apparent person cannot survive. What most people are not aware of is the driving force that is before hope, a driving force that fuels it. That driving force is the 'me' energy that wants to survive. The 'me' energy is made of the sense of lack and not being satisfied. It needs hope in order to keep seeking. The me energy imagines or dreams that, "If I solve this problem," "If I get a bit more money," "If I become fit and healthy," "If! Then I will be happy."

"Just a little bit more, a little bit more." This is the hope that apparent humanity runs on.

'Me' can't see this because 'me' is already in the next moment.

This is an extreme message for the apparent person.

What I am pointing to is that there is nothing in the next moment. There is nothing in hope.

I am pointing to hope being the dream.

Hope--the little bit more, is animating the dream, and although this dream is appearing this way, it can't be wrong.

Time

As soon as separation happens, time happens.

You are taught that you are an individual person moving through time and space, living your own life, and moving toward the future. That's how we learn. But soon, an idea comes in and is reinforced that says, "I am somebody here and everybody else is outside there."

Since birth we were taught that there is a past, present and a future. For example, right now maybe sitting is happening, reading is happening, but, the apparent person thinks, "I am sitting and reading a book." When the 'I' appears, then time starts.

This, what is, is actually **timeless**--where sensation is happening and everything is actually coming from nothing.

What Is, is timeless, and in timelessness, everybody, everything is simply just appearing.

It's only the human that lives in time and only the human that lives from the past to now. Animals do not live in space-time. But the past memory is appearing as what is; the future imagination is also appearing as what is.

Life as it is, is simply appearing in no time.

In the dreamlike reality, hope means that the dream continues.

- Naho -

I am often asked if what a person is doing is right or wrong. My answer to that is always the same: there is no wrong or right. This message is beyond the human reality of right and wrong, good and bad.

Whatever is happening is life and it can't go wrong.

The reason people ask this question is because they just don't know and they want to hold on to something. They feel lost. They want confirmation that they are okay.

You can't go wrong.

Following are questions to Naho during a live setting.

Personal

The seeming reality is so real for the apparent person, it does not exist outside the dualistic reality.

Ultimately, there is no problem. Whatever is happening is a perfect expression, but the seeming problem comes when 'it's happening to 'me'.

Question: So, the problem is mine?

Naho: All problems can only be personal, but there is no personal which ultimately means there is no problem. We humans think we are sharing experience but nobody ever shared experience.

Identification

Question: Are you talking about a dis-identification with the mind?

Naho: There is nobody that can identify with it.

Question: Most people are constantly identified with their mind, right?

Naho:. That's what they believe. **You** are the illusion.

Identification is who you think you are (somebody) which does not exist. The apparent personal reality is based on, "I exist." There is nothing wrong with this functioning but it does create a divided apparent reality.

Avoidance

Question: So many teachers teach the fixing of the character. What is your opinion of that?

Naho: That's perfect if that is what is seemingly happening. Trying to fix it happens.

You feel fulfilled by fixing but it is not going anywhere. What is wanted is to avoid the uncomfortableness that is driving the fixing.

I am Consciousness?

Question: Naho I have heard you ask the question recently to someone, you said, "Is it true that you remain unchanging, is it true that you are constant?" and there was something in that for 'me', I feel.

Naho: People think they are in a state of 'I am' and Being; they are somebody who can watch the changes (witness), but, there is actually only one appearance; there is nobody separate from this.

Question: So, I think that I can see that I am in an idea of being consciousness. Somehow when I am sitting with you, though, it seems to disappear.

Naho: A lot of seekers think that something unchanging is them. They recognize that something unchanging is who they are. People think that "I am awareness," but awareness is another *thing* that appears.

Question: Somehow I can notice this as true because I don't seem to be functioning from consciousness awareness now.

Naho: This is not a state nor a place, **you don't exist.**

All words come from nothing.

No words are the truth, only Silence.

All words come from nothing,
which ultimately means nothing, only pointing.

- Naho -

Unconditional Love

Question: What is unconditional love?

Naho: It's the only thing you are longing for because it does not exist in the human reality. Unconditional love is always already here. You don't have to go anywhere, you don't have to do anything. It's calling you to wake up from your personal dream.

Life

Question: As you say, appearances cannot wake up. If I can never wake up, then who is really hearing this?

Naho: It's nobody hearing. Life is pointing and life is hearing.

This is the end of 'me' and 'you'. This is the end of the person. There is only life and life is simply happening.

The sounds and voices appearing from nothing.

Everything and Nothing

Question: I hear you saying everything and nothing; what does that mean?

Naho: It's just the way it is. There is nothing to understand. It's not dualistic. The apparent person tries to see it when it can't be seen.

Loneliness

Question: I feel lonely. Is it important to have someone show me that there is nothing to see?

Naho: There is nothing wrong with the feeling of loneliness, but it comes from the sense of being somebody separate from life.

Who is going to show who? There's nobody inside the body. All appearances are appearing and appearance has no control.

Doership

Question: If there is no path and there is no one that follows it, there's nothing to do. My problem is that I have this feeling that I have to do something to reach a point. Sometimes this feeling is really annoying. I want to ask you what to do, but I guess there is nothing to do?

Naho: You want to avoid that feeling of lack or uncomfortableness because you feel you can't do anything from knowing there is no one having control. In the dream, seemingly there is a doer but it doesn't mean there is a doer, it just appears that way. It's not going to change anything.

You don't really want to reach a point; you want to feel comfortable. When there is an energetic dissolving, the question disappears because the need for answers disappears.

What you long for is beyond what to do or don't do. It is beyond that dynamic.

Nothing Sees

Question: When you say there is only this, are you pointing mainly at the level of the changing of appearances--saying there is only appearing and disappearing, however it appears right now?

Naho: It is what is.

This is the end of the one who knows. I am not giving you a meaning. I am not giving you anything to understand.

What I am pointing to is another possibility of another reality which has no separate knower.

Thought

Question: What about thoughts, are they still there, or are they more quiet for you?

Naho: If there is a thought, the thought is it. There is nothing more special than anything else. There is no problem with any thought.

When the 'me' is there, those thoughts are 'my' thoughts and they are seemingly happening to 'me'. It's just words.

Effort

Question: If there is a sense of an effort out of boredom, where is that sense coming from?

Naho: If an apparent effort happens for the character, there is nothing wrong with it, but if there is a trying to avoid an uncomfortable feeling or trying to get something to make 'me' feel better, that is all coming from separation.

There is always underneath, (whether it is noticed or not), a separate person having an agitation or feeling of not enough, something is not fulfilled.

That separation is only happening in the dream, but seemingly for the apparent person, it is really real; that makes you keep trying, efforting, seeking. Everything is happening on its own. There is never anyone doing anything.

"Just a little bit more, a little bit more." This is the hope that the apparent humanity runs on.

- Naho -

Using Nonduality

Question: When people hear nonduality, they start saying that there is no one; no one can make any decision. I don't know what to decide now. What can you say about that?

Naho: Nonduality can't be pulled into the dualistic world and used as information like a manual.

As a whole, separation and non-separation is the complete expression of wholeness. It is not that one is better than the other. The one who feels separate, naturally feels that no separation is better.

This message is extreme in that it does not lead anywhere. This message is expressing the way it is.

It is very simple.

Evolving

Question: Somehow, there seems to be progress, but the experience is not progress.

Naho: Exactly. Everything is apparent, both real and unreal but I am pointing to another reality. What we see in the human life, that is in time; progress is what is happening, but it is not real.

Everything comes from no-thing. One timeless being appearing as this.

It cannot be understood, it can't be known because nothing is separate from one being.

This, is incomprehensible.

Real Love

Question: What is the meaning of love for you?

Naho: Finding the meaning and purpose is completely dualistic, but very common. There is no meaning. Life IS love. There is only that.

For the person, love is often a relationship or feeling, or getting love from others, but that's only a feeling. Love is everything. In the apparent personal reality, the dualistic world, everything is conditional. People seek for unconditional love, but it does not exist in a conditional reality. People are preoccupied with finding love and they keep searching for it, but they actually don't know what they are looking for.

Real love is not something you need to try to keep. You don't even need to think about it.

True love is effortless.

Security

Question: What about survival, and the fear that goes along with it? Isn't it wired in our body?

Naho: Yes it is natural, this instinct, but it is also conditioning. For example, you were born in France and I was born in Japan, they are very different. But, that has nothing to do with the 'me' dynamic. After the 'me' is gone, the conditioning continues.

Question: There is a sense of worry here because the body is frail and is wired with the fear of dying, which has nothing to do with the 'me'.

Naho: Actually, that's the 'me' dynamic. For example, suddenly a truck comes and fear comes and naturally the body will try to protect itself, but you are talking about a mental worry.

In my story, I remember from an early age that I was a very sensitive child. When I was a 3 or 4 year old little baby, I told my mom that people are always scared. That's what I thought, because I was always afraid. Even if my family or friends were around, I would still feel agitation. The 'me' never ever has security. It lives in insecurity.

When 'me' dissolves, this is always security.

It is what is beyond the words that hears this message, beyond what you may want to figure out or leave behind.

- Naho -

Beliefs

Question: It seems like thoughts and beliefs are the problem, and we can't really stop it? Can't we just change the beliefs?

Naho: Apparent reality is apparently held together with ideas and concepts. When you start touching the natural reality, the beliefs or concepts can fall away, but it is not by somebody trying and or efforting. It happens on its own.

To change beliefs is still the dream.

What I am pointing to is beyond a need for change in beliefs.

What is beautiful about this message is that change can happen for the character but it's not something a character has done.

The World

Question: How do you react when you see all of the horrors of the world, the wars etc.? Are you affected by it, or do you just see it as an illusion?

Naho: Life can't be wrong. For the people that see the world as real, of course it is suffering and imperfect.

Question: You're saying you don't have any feelings about what's happening, any emotions?

Naho: Any emotion can arise. There is no seriousness added onto it.

There is nothing that sticks.

Consciousness

Question: People often talk about awareness and consciousness, they want to find out what consciousness is. If there is nothing I can do and I find that out, but consciousness remains, is that what I am? Am I consciousness?

Naho: Wanting to find out whether you are consciousness or not is still the dream. The truth as to whether you are consciousness or not really doesn't matter. Even if it is found out through experiences and having what you think is a final seeing (that you are consciousness), this becomes something to get; an object. Consciousness or awareness is now an object that has to be discovered, and that is the 'me' dream. Whatever 'me' finds is the dream.; that becomes the new reality. It reinforces the 'me' dream by saying that the 'me' can do something. When there are these big experiences, 'me' thinks it has found something. The apparent 'me' thinks 'me' is enlightened.

Awareness means that there is something that is aware of something else. That would mean that an object is there with something aware of it. That would mean two.
All of this is seemingly happening, but it comes from nothing.

Spiritual Experience

Question: From this observation there is nothing to do. Somehow, I gave up. There is like a river flowing that is opened. For some time it was very bitter when I realized that I had done everything and it didn't work. It's a sort of capacity that I don't know how it works that each time I give up there is an opening. This body has become charged with this huge spaciousness and then it will close up again. It feels almost like seasickness.

Naho: With spiritual experiences, anything can arise. I'm sure a lot of people here have had many awakenings. I'm not sure that these experiences will lead to what I am talking about. What I am pointing to is not a personal experience. It's the end of the person who cares about experiences. The 'me' dynamic will always claim a spiritual experience as theirs. It is not leading to something. Experiences are like a recognition of another reality. In a way, for that apparent

person, it is positive, but it is not what you
are looking for.

Peace

Question: Where is the peace?

Naho: Everywhere. Peace is natural. The peace that the 'me' is looking for is a feeling or comfort.

'Me' thinks 'me' is real, and the body is what I am. Everything to the 'me' becomes a solid thing.

There is no separation. There is nowhere to get too. There is no next moment.

Question: But you are knowing this. You appear peaceful.

Naho: I don't know. It's nothing to do with a feeling. It sounds like I know many things, or that I have some peace but this is the end of the one who needs peace.

Already Is

Question: So, if there is no separation, do you mean like embracing everything?

Naho: No, no. It is just as it is, already completion. Nobody is here embracing. It doesn't require someone to know there is only completion.

Nothing can see this because there is nothing separate from wholeness.

Question: Hard stuff.

Naho: Easiest. This is the most natural thing. It sounds really negative for the 'me' but this already is.

Question: It is like it doesn't matter if the fish swims left or right, it is in the water?

Naho: Yes. Nothing matters. Nothing is special, and everything is it.

Right and wrong are equally appearing, but for the 'me', right and wrong means something.

Relating

Question: It seems like there's a conversation happening between us two people, isn't that happening?

Naho: Seemingly happening, but there are not two people; communication seemingly happens without somebody.

Everything is simply happening.

Question: Is it still allowed for another body-mind system to feel personal love even when it is seen that it's only apparent?

Naho: Okay or not is not what this is about. Everybody wants to personalize, but there is no person in there. It's completely impersonal. If loving is happening then that is what's happening. It's the person that thinks, "This is my experience," that falls away.

Question: So the impersonal can appear as personal and say things like, "I love you?"

Naho: That can appear, but that is still impersonal and it doesn't belong to someone.

Question: It's such a beautiful paradox.

Naho: Yes.

Question: So the apparent separation feels like the loss of love?

Naho: Yes. It's a feeling of being lost from home. It's a looking for the home, but actually is home. Everything is so full and you can never be lost.

Question: You have made it difficult then to ask you any questions. There are no more questions left.

Naho: [Laughter]

Knowing

Question: Would you say that there is a knowing?

Naho: The 'me' thinks 'me' is knowing and that is separation. This is unknowing. Talking about this happens, but it's still impossible to talk about.

Question: So we really can't get rid of the 'me' can we? No one can get rid of the 'me'?

Naho: Me might have the idea, "I want to die," but me itself is an energy that wants to survive.

Layers

Question: Usually they say that there is awareness, that something is aware or has clarity and that it can be practiced. It sort of makes it a better prison?

Naho: It seemingly feels better in the dream. Staying in awareness and clarity happens, but it is still the dream which is uncomfortable; it is not completely satisfying. It may not even be noticed because it feels a little bit better. The person gets excited about that and they think this exercise works. At some point, it's going to feel like you are stuck, it will continue and never end, that dynamic.

Idea of Freedom

Question: This is where I get caught up: there's an awareness that there is no process but at the same time there's a story about a character who went through a process, and now I feel that enlightenment is nothing, and there is now freedom in that.

Naho: What is happening there is attaching to another reality and then coming back in the dream. It has nothing to do with your feeling of enlightenment. You are looking at freedom as a belief. Freedom is all of it.

Question: It feels like what we are talking about has no room for anything. I can't even put a drop of a story in anything.

Naho: People believe they can change their life story but people are the dream character which is the dream itself.

Question: You are saying that this has no purpose and it is not happening for anybody?

Naho: Yes.

Question: But there is a story in mind that there is, [laughs] and that's the 'joke'.

Naho: This is a crazy joke.

Nothing ever happened.

Free Will and Choice

Question: If there is no free will and choice, it means that everything is out of control, and everything is in freefall?

Naho: Yes, but there is nobody experiencing that, there is nobody controlling, and nobody being controlled.

Question: So, no one is ever born?

Naho: Yes. Identification with the body was born and becomes an energetic story of 'me'.

Question: So you are saying that I was not a child?

Naho: What is actually happening is that nothing is continuous. Everything is simply happening and not happening. This, is timeless.

Question: Sometimes this brings up fear because it feels it is about dying.

Naho: Yes, yes. People hear this message and a lot of fear happens. A lot of things happen to the body too-- reactions.

People have the fear of dying because they believe, "I am living, I exist."

Question: So then you are saying THIS is the end of the person?

Naho: Yes. It is the end of identification.

Question: The fact that this body is different from your body is not proof of separation being real? The world of forms?

Naho: No. That is the strongest belief, that, "I am here, and the world is outside." That is a strong sense.

Question: Would you then say that the person becomes the witness, like in the background?

Naho: No, no. Where is the background?

Question: So it's not about being detached from somewhere?

Naho: No. That would be two that can do witnessing. There is just one. Everything comes from nothing and is falling back to nothing. This has nothing to do with understanding, nothing to do with imagination, nothing to do with awareness. Somehow though, we believe there is something more, and that something is going to happen in the future to make my life better.

Beyond the Dream

Question: Is there anything at all in what you are saying that will help me? Is there something to get that can help ease the suffering? Is there a way to put an end to this suffering?

Naho: The difficulty in being an apparent individual is that we are always wondering if something will be useful or not. When you listen to this message, it is natural that you wonder if this is useful for 'me', but actually, this message is not useful for the apparent person.

This message is pointing to another reality, another possibility which is beyond the human reality.

Beyond the Words

Question: Hi Naho, I struggle with depression and anxiety. I am confused with the changes that seem to be happening. When I watch your videos, it's as if I can no longer hear too much of what you are saying, but it seems as if changes are happening on their own. I am feeling much better now, but I still don't understand how that is happening?

Naho: This message is beyond the intellect. The power of this message is beyond the words. When you hear this message, there is something knowing already that there is another reality which never left and to which you long for. It is not you that knows it, it is beyond all understanding, beyond the words. Something knows what is being pointed to, but the 'me' cannot find it. The moment the 'me' relaxes is when that energy is seemingly being touched.

Naturally

Question: Are you saying that there is no one looking through your eyes?

Naho: Yes, there is no one.

Question: What then, is looking through the eyes?

Naho: Nobody. We try to understand this through concepts and the intellect, but that is impossible and it has nothing to do with it.

Question: Do you feel a caring for others now?

Naho: Caring naturally happens. There is nobody here to see anyone, but caring naturally appears.

Nothing Dies

Question: Does life cease at the death of the body?

Naho: Do you mean the personal life?

Question: Yes.

Naho: Yes.

Question: Do the sensations cease?

Naho: That's what you believe because you believe you are inside of the body. That is why when the body dies, you believe you are going to die. But actually, nobody was ever born and nobody ever dies. There is only one being--the body is only an appearance. When the body dies, life continues. The apparent body dies, but nothing changes.There is no death. It is an apparent change which is simply one thing to another.

Question: You say that life continues, but will you be aware of it? If your body dies, how can you still see life? This causes me fear.

Naho: Because you believe you are inside the body. You believe that you are seeing life. Actually, there is nobody who sees life. Life is appearing as your body, but life cannot be possessed. The apparent person thinks, "This is my body," "This is my perception," and you don't want to lose it, and that is why fear comes. But actually, you never had any of it in the first place. Nothing is yours.

That dreamlike life then becomes so heavy. It is because we have invested so many years in identification,"It is all for 'me'," 'me' is the most important thing. The entire life has been invested for 'myself'.

Life is effortless.

Waking Dream

Question: You compare this situation with a dream, but there is quite a difference with real dreams. This here is fitted, real, lively and the night time dreams are dreams.

Naho: Yes, that's what you believe. When you wake up in the morning, you say, "Oh wow, that was a nice dream." You believe you suddenly come into the real world, but actually, that is still in the dream. But this dream is so convincing, so real, it's nearly impossible to see that 'this' is a dream.

Question: We have the impression that there is choice and time. If I decide to take off my watch, I am free to take it off or not.

Naho: Yes.

Question: So then, I am in control or not?

Naho: Not. But seemingly in time, in the dream, there is apparent cause and effect that appears. For example, if you drop a thing, it may break. Life appears as cause and effect but it is only because life is appearing as that; that doesn't mean that there is cause and effect. You think you have control because life is appearing as you taking off the watch, but that idea appears, it is not you creating it. It feels like it, but where did that come from?

As a child, when we looked under a microscope and we saw only atoms, of which scientists have discovered amounts to nothing.

Question: We build quite a complicated dream.

Naho: Ooh la la, yes. Everything is like a story.

Young children know this. When the baby is born, there is nothing there that knows that it is there, but we are taught that we are the person. Everyone is living like that! It is because we were so convinced through life of this that it becomes energetic, it becomes a feeling. "I am this body."

Effortless

Question: Naho, I am what is called a seasoned seeker, I have done it all. Many experiences, and one awakening around 10 years ago. I saw at that time that I could not ever get this in any way, that it just happened. I found myself doing these practices in order to make the 'me' smaller, or so I was told. It seemed in my experience of listening with you, that it is happening on its own and something has relaxed here without any effort. I feel that what these teachers are doing with people is nearly the opposite to what should be happening?

Naho: What I am pointing to is that efforting and changing and doing practice reinforces the 'me' because the idea of 'me' having control becomes real. It is going round and round in the 'me' dream. You will never find the exit.

The dream teachers sincerely think they are doing the best thing.

What I am saying has nothing to do with giving you a practice. I am pointing out the dynamic of a separate reality, which creates a personal suffering--which is the dream.

Apparent change happens naturally.

Powerful

Question: There's a sense that the 'me' is sometimes more dissolved or not dissolved. There's also an awareness of that being a story too but it seems to be what is appearing?

Naho: It seems to be happening. What enlightenment is, is that all illusion disappears. When the person is experiencing life through time, what is happening is real to the 'me' energy. At the end, when everything is gone, what is seen by nobody is that everything was an illusion. In the apparent time, it feels like less of a 'me' or less contraction, but in the end, nothing ever happened. For the person, it feels so real, but that part is illusion. It seems to be happening, but it is not real. Nothing ever happened. That seeing also disappears.

Question: Is there a story behind the Naho 'me' energy that existed and is no longer here?

Naho: In the story, we could say that Naho existed before, then Naho is gone, but actually, Naho never existed; Naho never seeked. It's not happening. There is no sense there was somebody here. There is nobody.

Absolute Freedom

Question: Many people ask the question, "Who are you," I would like to ask you, who are you?

Naho: There is nothing.

People think that everything is separate and that is why that question comes up. You believe that you are somebody.

Question: You won't say, "I am awareness," or "I am consciousness." ?

Naho: No. People might use those words, and here I might use the word, 'life', or 'oneness', anything can be used, but it is not important. There is no meaning. There is one thing appearing as this. The people want to know who we really are because they believe, "I have a life, I exist." If there is only one life, appearing as this, then nobody ever had anything or is anything.

Question: I am not saying that there is an I and awareness, there is just awareness, but I'm not sure.

Naho: No, you don't know. Nobody knows. What is happening is all there is.

The person who wants to know about awareness or consciousness is still wanting to hang on to something. The person wants to know who we really are which is a beautiful story. Finding out our true nature is a beautiful story, but who can know that?

Thoughts are appearing and knowledge is happening but when it disappears, it's gone.

Nothing can be kept. It is opposite to what you think you want, but that is the freedom.

No Center

Question: When you live out of nonduality, is there no more mask necessary?

Naho: Nonduality is not a way of living. Nonduality points out there there is no center that is living life.

There is nothing to protect, no mask to wear even though the basic functioning of the apparent person happens.

Nobody's Experience

Question: During deep meditation, there was an experience of nothing and everything and there was fulfillment. During this time, I did not want to seek. What does the mean?

Naho: Yes. It means you were not there.

Question: Is it possible to get to this state?

Naho: No. You were not there to get it. You did not experience it. That fulfillment arose because you were not there. The 'you' came back and you felt you lost it. But actually, nobody experienced it. You owned that experience. "That happened to 'me'." It didn't happen to anybody.

Impersonal

Question: I hear so many teachers say how enlightenment is only for 1 percent of the population and super rare. I'm not convinced anymore that any of this can happen here.

Naho: The apparent seeker is taking the hopelessness personally and then get more and more depressed. That is not how the message is meant to be.

Question: It seems to 'me' that you are very much at ease.

Naho: There is nobody here that can be at ease. There is nobody here having a positive experience. It is the end of the person who cares about it. It is not personal. Ease or not ease. It is not personal.

Realization

Question: So you are saying that this is a strong illusion that seems to be so real?

Naho: Yes.

Question: And we are deeply believing it?

Naho: Yes, but nobody is believing it.

Question: This is a joke?

Naho: Yes.

[Much laughter]

Poetry

Life Is

One, appearing as many.

From an apparent person, it can't be seen.

Apparent people compare with others.

They see the world, good or bad, right or wrong, better or worse.

But actually,

it's one and the same thing, looking from a different angle.

Life is simple, as it is.

If life looks complicated, it's because you're looking through dualistic eyes.

Life is simply as it is.

Importance

There is no importance anywhere.

As soon as the word importance is heard,

it sounds as if there is something important that exists.

When you start to work on your own importance, that creates a tension that is not so obvious....

Importance doesn't always create security or freedom; its effects might also be of anxiety, worry and seriousness.

Importance only exists in the apparent human dream.

Life is always free and secure without having any importance.

Life is an expression, it has no meaning.

Life is Love

Do you know why?
Because it is the essence of all there is.
Nothing is appearing as many,
it appears as different forms,
it changes.
There is one thing that never changes
and that is the essence of all there is.
The whole world
is made
of love.
Whatever is seemingly happening,
it is always in love.
Love is all there is.

Longing

There is only love.
Unconditional love is all there is.
When the apparent person appears, it begins
to search for love which is never lost.
This searching for love by
getting something,
avoiding something or
changing something to something else,
is covering up the love
which is never lost.
The love you ever long for can't be found in
seeking in the next moment.
But
one day, suddenly the energy of seeking for
love
can vanish.
When this dynamic, which hides the love
you long for--stops,
Then
what is left is unconditional love
which is always already here.
The love you long for is before you seek.

Conclusion

Originally, this text had 266 pages, but I wanted something that goes straight to the point so we cut many words.

This book will not offer an intellectual stimulation, but may, in one sentence, reveal a whole other reality since what you long for is not in the words nor in understanding.

What this is pointing to is not in concepts or ideas but beyond what you imagine or know.

This, is everything and it never left you.

Who you think you are is always in and as love.

Although this is all coming from nothing to nothing, there is nothing that needs to be changed.

May you find that you melt between the lines.

Love,

Naho

Index

NOTES

Notes

Notes

NOTES

So in love with this message. Passion is arising from nothing, for nobody, and going back to nothing. Love is expressing itself; love is all there is.

- Naho -

Printed in Poland
by Amazon Fulfillment
Poland Sp. z o.o., Wrocław

59952812R00063